Leadership: It's Child's Play

Ten Steps to Children's Leadership Development:
A Guide to Leadership

Written by Taylor Wilson Thompson

Library of Congress Control Number: 2013909758

Printed in the United States of America

Leadership: It's Child's Play
Ten Steps to Children's Leadership Development:
A Guide to Leadership

ISBN-13: 978-0-615-82178-8

For more information about the
Taylor Wilson Thompson Family Fund,
please visit twtff.org

Acknowledgments

I have so many people who I need to thank for helping me bring
"Leadership: It's Child's Play" into fruition:

My parents have been my rock through all of this. They have always been there to encourage, nurture and support me in all that I do. They have always encouraged me to do my best and never take my blessings for granted. They have allowed me to grow and have experiences that have helped to shape me in positive ways. I can't thank them enough for everything they do for me.

All of my friends have been my biggest fans throughout the years. They offered me advice and gave me encouragement that helps me every day. The consistency of their friendship is rare; it gives me confidence and I appreciate it greatly.

My teachers along the way who provided me with knowledge and skills that allow me to think rationally and solve problems in logical and thoughtful ways. They, along with my parents, instilled within me the belief that if you work hard, anything is possible.

Finally, my fifth grade teacher Ms. Street. She has taught me so much, cheered me on and has always been there for me. She taught me the rudiments of learning and instilled within me a desire to continue to grow academically, socially and morally. More than anything, she has always been there as a friend, willing to talk to me and share advice. I thank her for being that special person in my life.

A Note From the Author

I'm Taylor Wilson Thompson, founder of the Taylor Wilson Thompson Family Fund and author of *Leadership: It's Child's Play: Ten Steps to Children's Leadership Development.* Over the past year I have been working to write this book in order to spread awareness of young people's abilities to take charge and lead, and to share what I have learned about leadership and leading a group.

In this book, I share my opinion on our society today and caution that we are educating our youth in a fashion that implies that what they learn today is only applicable to our society in the future, rather than at the present. On the contrary, I believe that once an individual is able to communicate their ideas, feelings, knowledge and expertise, their perspective is valid and relevant for the common good. As such, individuals are able to lead and make change at any age.

To accentuate this point, in my book, I chose to share with you a story of my fourth-grade self and my friend's quest to improve our playgrounds' condition. In this true story, I account the things that I learned and understood from a very young age and relate it to what I have come to understand and apply in my everyday life, in my steps toward leadership development.

This book is incredibly important to me because it has helped me grow, as well as learn. Before founding the Taylor Wilson Thompson Family Fund, I would not have imagined that I could write a book at fifteen, or have enough to say to actually finish the book. But, as I look at my finished work, it makes me realize what is possible. Also, it makes my passion for making a change in our society even more fervent. If I can impact just one person through the leadership training and educational awards that I fund, or the book that I have written to make a difference in our society, I would gauge it as a tremendous success.

Taylor Wilson Thompson

Foreword

A few years ago my wife and I attended the award ceremony at my daughter's elementary school. Unbeknownst to us, she was being given the fourth-grade Leadership Award. During the ceremony, my wife and I looked on in amazement, as her teacher extolled the rare talents of all the young people present. The students were being celebrated as true twenty-first-century leaders, capable of making a meaningful difference in the world. Taylor's teacher, Mrs. Rhodes, chronicled how they had all come to her as single-digit learners, wide-eyed neophytes in the ways of middle school. Now, they were developing into world changers capable of so much more than anyone could imagine.

The various awards were handed out to students for citizenship, community service, academics, musical acumen, and the like. Concluding the ceremony was the presentation of the award for leadership. When our daughter's name was read aloud, my wife and I grew emotional as we watched Taylor rise with the grace we had taught her and approach the stage. We chuckled as we watched her balance on her one-and-one-half-inch heels, and wondered at how rapidly she was growing up.

Mrs. Rhodes handed Taylor a brightly embossed certificate and a plaque embossed with her likeness on the left panel of the award. On the right panel were framed words celebrating her leadership skills.

After the presentation, our daughter thanked all who were present for attending this ceremony. Then she too, in celebratory praise, spoke of the ambitious agenda the middle-schoolers had before them. She concurred with her teacher that there was "so much more these young minds were capable of doing if they were simply given more tools and broader opportunities to do so." I listened to her as she told one adult, "I am so glad to have received the award. But all the students here are talented. Just give us time and we will make our marks in the world." My wife and I laughed under our breath. Who were these children that they should think so highly of themselves?

After a commemorative ice cream and cake fest at the local ice-cream shop, we talked with our daughter about the past year and why she thought she had won the award. She told us that leadership was not a big deal. "It's not hard. You just figure out what and where you want to go, or what you want to do. Then you get people to go with you." Then she said something that stuck with us. "You know, leadership, it's child's play."

She described to us the moment when she realized that leadership was about just moving the needle, pushing the envelope and getting people to do things that were in the group's best interest. She said her watershed moment came when the fourth-grade girls had their bake sale to raise money for the playground. Against all odds, they did the impossible: they raised money, enthused students and teachers and made the playground better.

So we suggested Taylor think about writing about her experience to create a guide for parents and teachers. Perhaps her words could inspire other young people to take the lead and inspire adults to give students the space to practice their budding leadership skills.

This small book is her reflection on that experience and her current take on leading and leadership. Hope you enjoy it.

Dr. Donald E. Thompson

Contents

Contents

The Story

A few years ago, when I was in the fourth grade, my girlfriends and I were outside on the playground doing our usual stay-away-from-the-boys exercises, all the while attempting to get their attention. (Our mothers continue to tell us that at some time they will be important to us. We don't quite know when this will happen, but we are hedging our bets.)

We noticed that the swing-sets, jungle gyms, and other playground equipment were in really bad shape. There was chipped paint and rust everywhere and jagged corners on the slides. It wasn't safe. Even the school colors of azure blue and white covering the swings seemed secondary to the brownish orange rust cascading from the top of the swing standards to the bottom, where they were nestled into the pitted clay and gravel soil.

The equipment was in such bad shape that at recess we were forced to spend our time playing "gaga" with the boys or, worse yet, football or other ruffian games aimed at maiming and hurting the human body. We wondered in amazement why no one had called attention to the condition of the playground equipment. Didn't they care about us?

How could we be expected to grow and develop into ladies without the proper venues for getting our "gossip on" and talking about the latest happenings on Disney and MTV? Not to mention the time spent worrying about scraping, scarring, or snagging our bodies on the outdoor playground equipment. Worse yet, how were we expected to get the demanding exercise needed to maintain these quickly maturing bodies of ours? Something needed to be done.

We wondered why the adults hadn't done something about it. Why didn't they just fix the equipment? Was it that they hadn't noticed? Here we were enjoying the last few years of freedom before we arrived at the dreaded middle school and now we were faced with a problem that was not of our making and clearly someone else's responsibility. We wondered, how could our teachers, mentors, and protectors allow us to be in harm's way? It was clear to us that we had to do something about it—we had to act!

My dad says if you are going to solve a problem, solve it at the highest level. I heard his words ringing in my ears: "Don't waste your time seeking help from someone who cannot give it to you." Using that advice, I suggested to my friends that we needed to bypass the custodian, nurse, teacher assistants and teachers. I convinced them that we needed to go directly to the top. That afternoon, I made an appointment to see the principal.

I felt that if we initially brought it to the attention of our teacher, we would have a class meeting, and then the topic would go to the student council. The student council would put it on the agenda, and because fourth-grade girls had thought of the idea, the playground matter would get shoved to the back of the agenda and never be discussed. But, if it were discussed, it would eventually have to go to a faculty meeting; then to a parents' meeting; and then back to us sometime in the spring. That wouldn't do.

We made the request for a meeting with the principal and on Monday, she graciously accepted, scheduling it for later in the week. On Tuesday, my girlfriends and I met to go over the strategy. We decided we should be straight-forward and just set out our concerns by showing her the articles we had pulled from the Internet. Also, we would tell her what we had observed while watching kids play and how afraid we were for them. We wanted to discuss injuries to children while playing on poorly equipped playgrounds. We would talk about medical concerns associated with rust, blood poisoning and staph infections. Finally, we would provide her with a reasonable list of supplies and replacement equipment that could remedy the playground situation. We knew Mrs. Jamison to be a reasonable woman. How could she not understand our concerns.

On Wednesday, we arrived in the main office promptly after school dismissal at 3:15 p.m. We sat down in the principal's waiting room and nervously awaited the call into the darkened dungeon lair affectionately called the principal's office.

Mrs. Jamison never turned on the ceiling lights in her office. Some say it is because she wanted to peer more deeply into the eyes of frightened students as their pupils expanded, seeking out a light source as she metes out her punishment. We walked into the office, and I wondered aloud whether there was enough light to see anything in there.

Mrs. Jameson stood as we entered, urging us to come in and have a seat. We looked at each other, remembering all the horror movies we had seen and wondering if we were in one. Although Mrs. Jamison was an attractive woman, the moment evoked memories of the wicked witch in Snow White. We looked for fruit. What in the world were we doing here? Had we lost our minds? We had volunteered to go see the principal. Were we crazy?

In her office were two guest chairs, but that was plenty for the four of us who had nervously entered into this crypt of darkness to utter our request. In order to maintain a cohesive look, we positioned ourselves on the corners of two chairs, two people to a seat. It may have looked funny, but we braced ourselves in a line that couldn't be broken.

Mrs. Jamison listened carefully to our supplications; she nodded at the right times, acknowledging our concerns. We handed her our research, neatly arranged in a pink folder. She accepted it and smiled graciously. After we laid out our request for the equipment to be repaired, she moved forward in her chair, placed her hand on her chin and gave us that "this is interesting" look of hers.

Because of her smile and pensive gaze, we were convinced she would bend to our logic and grant our request. But the look on her face went from supportive to apologetic.

"Sorry, girls, there is just no money in this year's school budget to accomplish the things you want to have done. Maybe next year," she said.

We all looked at each other, not knowing what to say. We were apoplectic in our facial contortions; we squirmed in spastic motions. She asked if we needed a bathroom break.

How could there be no money? Our parents paid tuition. We know this because they were always reciting to us, "Do you know how much this school costs?" The school was always announcing some new fundraiser, and there had just been a silent auction in the gym last week. How could there be no money? Had someone stolen it? Had they lost it in the stock market? We could not believe our ears; we had not been prepared for that reply. We left confused and brokenhearted; we were more appalled than dejected.

The resolve of our "fantastic four" evaporated into thin air. Slumped shoulders, refracted faces with worry lines not becoming of such young faces pushed back crested tears. All of us tried to hide the disappointment. It was useless. Preteen tears rolled down our cheeks, until the first gasp and sob was heard. I tried to rally the other three into believing that there is always a way to accomplish our goals. It was a lost cause. Paraphrasing one of my dad's favorite blues singers, B.B. King, "the thrill was gone."

When I got home, I told my parents what happened. I shared with them the grief we felt upon hearing there was no way to get the equipment repaired. I reemphasized how unsafe and dangerous the playground seemed and expressed my concern for my safety and that of the other kids. I showed them the plan we had written up, including the graphs and charts we painstakingly copied at the library. I chronicled the most meaningless event at our meeting in order that they might feel our pain.

I told them I didn't agree with the feelings of my friends that all was lost. "There has to be a way to get this done," I said. They looked at me and told me, "Then do something about it!" I thought it was kind of cruel to tell your ten-year-old daughter to fix a problem adults had allowed to happen. But then I remembered who I was and in whose house I had lived for the past ten years. Their response was consistent with their responses for more than a decade.

My parents have always treated me more like an adult than a child. When I was five, they would bring home situational problems from work. The issues ranged from problems with personnel to budgetary issues and what my dad called systems theory. My parents would ask me to give them my best advice on how to solve the problems at hand. I would wax eloquent with my sandbox philosophy, developed from many long days on elementary playgrounds in Bethesda, Maryland, and Kalamazoo, Michigan. Once I had given my answer, my parents would celebrate my logic and tell me my solutions were right on target. Little did I know they were priming me to think rationally and logically. They were showing me how to frame a problem and utilize reasoning skills to come up with workable solutions.

My parents always said to me, when there is a problem to be fixed, "lead and don't follow," "take charge when others will not," "make doing part of your dreaming," and finally, "if a ship is sinking, stop worrying, do something." So with that as a backdrop, I got started on my journey to get that playground fixed.

That night, my mother reminded me of Gandhi's words that I had used in a history paper, "Be the change you want to see in the world." I was set, nothing was going to deter me. We were going to fix the playground equipment; we would get the money; we would show the teacher, principal and parents that a group of fourth-grade girls were a force to be reckoned with.

The first step was to figure out what we really wanted to do, what we really wanted to accomplish. Should we get the entire playground fixed or should we do it in parts? Maybe we should just focus on a small portion we could manage. After much discussion, we decided not to try to figure out what we would tackle. We would just raise money and let the amount of money we raised determine what we could do. The next day, we made another appointment with the principal to discuss the fund raising we had in mind for the school.

The following Tuesday, we again gathered in the principal's office to meet with her. This time, the request was simple; we wanted to have a series of bake sales. We set our fund raising goal at six-hundred dollars. That was the amount we needed to buy new balls, ropes and nets for the playground and pay for paint to spruce up the swings, teeter-totters, and other stationary equipment. This was our first experience in fund raising; we had no idea whether or not that amount was easy or hard to get; and we just knew that was what we were going to do.

Mrs. Jamison was imaginatively surprised with our request for a second visit; and she was a bit taken aback by our presumptuousness in suggesting that we could do something the adults hadn't thought of doing.

Her coddling conversation was not demeaning, but not what we expected. She looked at us as four neophyte girls who had suggested something far above our abilities, and certainly above our pay grade. But her response strengthened our resolve to make this thing happen. Finally she said, "This might be possible. Let me look closer at your ideas. I will get back with you."

She gazed down for a second time at our plan and a smile embraced her face. She looked up and said, "You know girls, I think this might be a good idea. Why don't you try one bake sale and we will see how it goes."

As we were leaving, she stopped us outside in the hall and gave us a few pointers on what could be done and how, when and where the bake sale should take place. We knew we were well on our way to having the Dragon colors of azure blue and white wave brightly on the playground once again.

My friends and I had a number of meetings focused on plotting a strategy for the bake sale. Emotionally, we were perched between our anger pointed squarely at the adults, who had made a decision not to do anything about our playground, and getting back at them by raising money and flaunting it in their faces.

We talked about what we should sell, and we even talked about what we should wear during the sales. We were all over the place. Finally, I said, "Let's focus. We have to keep our minds on what it is we are trying to do and nothing else." My eyes narrowed and my left eyebrow arched, just like my mom's. They knew I was serious.

They were a little shocked to see me turn into the Evil Witch of the West, but I realized something at that moment I had not realized before: somebody must lead. In a group, someone has to take charge, keep the group on point, be the elephant in the room. I was that somebody. Under my breath I uttered, "Okay, world here I come. I can't tell you where I'm going, but here I come."

I remembered the times I had watched my mom when she was getting ready to go to a board meeting, take a deep breath and quote her one hundred and one year-old grandmother saying, "Let's make haste." That was her rallying cry when she knew the task ahead of her might be difficult. She knew that making difficult decisions were part of her job and that the decisions were important for the common good. But as she says, "You can't walk backwards if you're the one in front."

I thought about when my dad had to give a major speech or deliver bad news to agencies with whom he was consulting. He would stand in front of the mirror and mimic Roy Scheider in *All That Jazz* and say, "It's show time." So I took a deep breath, stood in front of the mirror, and said, "Make haste, it's show time." Then I fell on my knees and prayed for strength that I could handle this task.

I had an epiphany. For the first time, I saw the problem backwards. In my mind, I saw the task completed—the playground equipment was repaired, new equipment had been purchased and kids were playing and having fun. I imagined a mental model of what was possible; it was no longer a dream. It was a connect-the-dots problem. All I had to do was draw the lines to the points. Connect the dots. I could do that.

I had been concentrating on the problem and all the forces operating against us. I had been consumed by the prospect of all the things that could go wrong along the way: The adults would not take us seriously; parents would treat us like children and give us more advice than we needed or wanted. I spent an enormous amount of time, focused on how to deal with the varying personalities of ten and eleven-year-olds.

I focused on everything except the playground being finished. In my mind, I never saw it completed. I never had a real vision of what it was we were trying to accomplish. I never saw what we were working toward. In an instant, at just that moment, I saw the vision clearly. It was as if I looked through a wormhole in time and saw a parallel path. But this path was one that was reversed; it showed me the steps from the accomplished task back to the beginning. Seeing it that way allowed me to see the relationships between each of the connected parts. That path was clear and I saw the steps needed to accomplish the task.

I convened my friends and shared with them my newfound vision of the future. I told them that we could raise the money for the playground by having a series of bake sales, not just one. The probability of us raising six-hundred dollars in one day was not likely. So we had to plan a long-term strategy that would generate the money over several sales. My friends reminded me that the principal had authorized us to have just one sale. I told them the first sale would be so successful, she would want us to have another.

We quickly realized that none of us were allowed by our parents to touch the stove, let alone the ovens. How could that be pulled off? We could buy the food; no one would have to cook. Oops, we didn't have jobs and none of us received more than seven dollars' allowance for the week—twenty-eight dollars wouldn't go very far in filling at least four tables full of gooey delights.

We committed to talk to our dads that night; they were soft touches and would do anything for their sweet little girls. We would indicate that we had the principal's blessing and we needed their help to pull off this business venture. We would get their approval and possibly a loan, gift, or grant of thirty dollars or more. Once they said yes to the idea and the financial commitment, we would crawl on their laps and get them to talk to mom about it. Getting the dads to commit was critical. We knew dads couldn't cook, but they loved their little girls, so they would be soft touches for money and they would run interference for us if anything got in the way. We knew they would be all in.

The next morning, we gathered at the sand box before school. Each of us was beaming—mission accomplished.

All dads were on board with the plan. The dads had talked to the moms and the moms wanted a family touch to the sale. They wanted to bake their specialty for the sale. This was more than we had ever dreamed. We had money to buy food and moms were baking, too. We would have enough food for six to seven tables.

At morning recess, we continued our planning. We concluded that if we dangled sweets in the face of five to twelve-year-olds, they would be immune to all rational thought. The only thing that would register in their minds would be the phrase "got to have it." So bake sale it was. How could this go wrong, we wondered?

I knew that everything takes planning, and although this seemed simple, the bake sale would take a lot of planning. At lunch we went outside and sat on the benches by the front doors of the school and began our first planning session. We had seen the principal and teachers sit there plenty of times while they were plotting evil things to do to us. So we felt there must be something special about that spot. We felt it was an adult spot because none of the kids ever sat there. So we sauntered out to the north bench, crossed our legs, tapped our feet and thought, just like we had seen the adults do.

What few new ideas we had were all over the place. This was no special spot. We couldn't figure out what we wanted to sell. Should the food be gooey? Should we buy it or have our parents make it? We soon all concluded that none of our parents had ever prepared baked goods for us at home. So we quickly surmised they could not cook well enough to warrant selling their products.

We recognized that we had to cater to the taste buds of the consumer. We had to account for the tastes of the students we were going to serve. What was it they wanted? What would tantalize their tongues into submission? "Step back and take a look at the goal," I said. "We have to make our decision based on what we want to earn to fix the playground. How do we maximize our time, resources and energies in order to gain a greater return on our product?" I said out loud, mimicking one of my mother's phone calls.

Surely, we weren't the first kids to have a bake sale as a way of trying to earn money for a school project. I suggested that we think about how adults pull off bake sales and maybe we could just pattern ours after theirs. That idea went over like a lead balloon. They accused me of thinking like an adult. "Let's just do it," they all said, citing a Nike mantra we all knew too well. However, feeling we did not need to invent a wheel that was already rolling down the hill, I did my own recognizance work on bakesalography.

That evening, I checked the "www" portals to gain a clearer view of what it takes to have a successful bake sale. Then I talked to kids from other schools and others at church that had bake sales and asked them about their experiences. I learned two things: 1) Make sure you have food that is bright, sticky, and bigger than one hand can hold. Kids are visual and tactile. More than aroma, kids need to view the pastries as attractive. It must be something they would not get at home and that their mothers would look upon with disapproval. 2) Keep parents, teachers and the principal away from the food table; they drive away customers.

Most of the research indicated that something always goes wrong during the first bake sale. There is an unexpected event, such as the food not arriving on time or, worse, there is a fire drill. So we decided to have a test run just to see if we had all the bases covered. We pretended to line up the tables and made believe there were students lined up and we were serving them. Finally, we all celebrated the idea that the money needed was all made in one sale. This dry-run event helped to get the team on task.

The days leading up to the sale were excruciating. Almost every hour there were phone calls, texts, and emails from my anxious teammates lamenting the decision we had made to go forward with the sale. What if no one comes? What if the students have no money? What if someone steals the money? What if the boys sabotage the sale?

I slapped myself just to get out of my self-imposed negative stupor. Finally, I said, "Come on, we are all smart kids with a great idea. We can do this. No one has confidence in us but we have confidence in ourselves."

The week before the sale, I made phone calls to my teammates to make sure they were not having second thoughts. They were. Now my task was to ease the fears of the fearful who a few days ago were full of conviction. I decided to overload them with positive communication. I was going to overload them with positive messaging in hopes of buoying their spirits. Twice a day, I sent a group email suggesting to them new and creative ways of moving the project on, lifting their spirits.

One way of giving them hope was to make sure they were part of the action. They had to be busy making things happen. So we divided up the tasks of making flyers, getting the aprons for the tables, getting the cash drawer, cleanup and selling the merchandise. Each of them had a role in the success of the sale. I told them that if any of them failed to complete their task, the whole mission would fail. Each of their tasks was critical to our success and each of them was positively indispensable.

Finally, the day of the bake sale arrived. There was an eerie relief because I no longer had to hold hands with the doubters—they were so busy focusing on their assigned tasks that doubting was not an option. As the hour drew near to a close our hands were drenched with perspiration and our parched throats grew hoarse as we whispered suggestions through six hours of the school day. I knew I had to maintain my cool and lead in the face of my fears. At 2:45 p.m., I looked up and said, "Make haste. It's show time."

We trouped out of our classroom and down the seemingly longer-than-usual hallway to the table arranged in the corridor by the exit door. We were thankful that the principal had arranged for the custodian to set the tables out early. We figured if we got the students while they were leaving, it would be like the checkout lane in the grocery store and they couldn't resist us. We waited breathlessly for the final second to tick by before the students left their classrooms.

Alum led the way as he burst from the fourth-grade classroom to the table splayed with sweets, succulents, and other confectionary treats. While one of the girls did bake chocolate chip cookies with her mom, everyone else brought cookies, cakes, and muffins from the city's best bakeries. Alum, Mark, Sean, and Jenna purchased half of table #1. Table two was wiped out in the first three minutes. We looked up after serving the first patrons and saw a line that stretched more than forty strong. I mumbled under my breath and paraphrased a movie quotation from Roy Scheider, in the movie *Jaws*, "we're going to need a bigger table."

The kids came in droves; we were flummoxed. This was too much. Could we handle it? Was there enough food? Who had the money? Word about the goodies spread to the fifth graders and then the sixth and seventh graders. They came with reckless abandon, pushing and shoving, shouting questions. "How much is the dragon cookie? What if I buy three of these, is there a better price? Can you hold this until I get some more money from my locker?" The eighth graders were far too cool to be among the throng, but I did see April and Samantha handing money to their younger brothers and sisters to get them something. This was great; it was surpassing our wildest imagination.

Within minutes, four of the five tables of food were gone but so were all but a few kids. What should we do now? How would we get rid of the rest of the food? I remembered the four-letter word. It is the only one my father knows when he is shopping—SALE.

Quickly, we fashioned a sale sign advertising all items half off. Heather paraded the sign around outside to tantalize the kids who were standing on the school porch and sidewalk waiting for their parents to pick them up.

Heads turned toward the sign and then toward the door of the lobby where one lone table still sat full of confections. We knew we had them when a second grader asked her mom for just one more cookie and her big sister did the same. Five minutes later, our eighteen-minute sale was over.

As the students finally left the building, parents ferried the fructose-filled bodies away and we knew they would be back for the second sale. Just sixty seconds past our first bake sale, we were developing a strategy for the second sale for the next week. We were building upon what we had learned from this sale. Our confidence was brimming.

We cleaned up the tables, swept the floor and wiped down the chairs that were now sticky with sugar crystals and powdered sugar. Mrs. Walker came over and told us how proud she was of our efforts. She said she never doubted us and whether we believed it or not, other teachers were hoping for our success. She hugged each of us and again said we were all leaders. We smiled as she walked away, hugged each other and went into the main office to count the money.

Bake sale number one was an amazing event and it netted us $235.98. We were on our way to reaching our goal. We grinned with glee; we gloried in our gargantuan success. How could others ever have doubted us? How could we have doubted ourselves?

We met with the principal. She, too, was pleasantly surprised by the success of the sale. She admitted that she was more impressed that we had pulled it off by ourselves. No adults helped set it up or clean up afterwards. She gave us permission to have sale number two and three. She said that whatever we were short after those sales, the school would make up to reach the six-hundred dollar goal.

Two sales later, we were pros at retail sales. We were ready to give advice on how to market, merchandise and dispose of unwanted goods. We knew how to assess the look in a buyer's eyes when she or he was in the throes of indecision. We mastered new inflections to the phrases "You know you want it" and "Can't you taste the after-taste?"

By the end of the third sale, we had raised $643.60. We actually surpassed our goal. Each of us had grown closer through our successes and we had overcome the demons of insecurity and fear. We knew it was possible to do great things if you have confidence and hope. We had the evidence of success in working as a team; we had reaped the benefits of trusting in the power of a group touching and agreeing on a single goal.

Who knew? We were tired and the bloom was off the rose. We didn't know how bakeries did it. This was a lot of work, but the work was fulfilling. In many ways, we were glad the sales were over. The principal called us into the office the morning after the last sale and indicated that the school would add money to our total in order to do even more to the playground than we desired.

A month after the last sale, the principal scheduled a special Saturday for kids, parents and staff to get together and have a Playground Clean-up and Refresh Day—Dragon Style.

The four of us, with the principal, were the first there on Saturday. We were all so excited to see the dream become a reality and we felt a kinship, knowing we had achieved what was deemed impossible in many others' eyes. We had made the impossible possible and found success where others imagined only failure.

As we cleaned the grounds, scraped rust off the equipment and applied Dragon blue and white paint to everything we could, it was a glorious day for all of us. It was a confirmation of what Gandhi said: "Be the change you want to see in this world."

Along the way, I learned a great deal about myself and what it takes to be a leader. I wanted to share what I learned with other kids, so they wouldn't be afraid to take the big step toward leadership and getting things done. I also wanted to share this with adults, so they would know and appreciate the power that lies in the heart and will of this ten-year-old, and their own kids.

After all, leadership, it's child's play.

Chapter 1

Seeing the Vision and Setting a Goal
You Can Reach

There is a Bible scripture that says, "Where there is no vision, the people perish…" (Proverbs 29:18 KJV). I have always thought that to be another one of those Bible verses I learned in chapel, and then had to recite at home. After all, I am a preacher's kid.

But after the experience of managing a bake sale to raise funds to repair the playground, I am a living testament to the fact that if you can see it, you can have it, and if you can't imagine it, you will never attain it.

Many don't take the time to truly examine the real possibilities. I am not sure if they are afraid of success or afraid of the responsibility associated with that success. However, I fear that many are not prepared for the work it takes to prepare for success or to make their dream a reality.

Some think if they are going to be a leader, they must imagine great things or have a vision that unveils the unknown. In reality, all that's necessary is to see something clearly from beginning to end. To see it, you must not be afraid of your creativity and you must not be afraid to think of things that others have not yet begun to imagine.

My leadership epiphany came when I stopped doubting my vision; I listened to my heart first and others second and took the time to believe in the possibility of my being successful. I saw the scaffolding of an idea and was able to build upon that scaffolding a concrete idea. I imagined a road map that led me back to the beginning tasks—my father calls that reengineering. Once I saw the structure, I began to see the way to get there.

Children are always dreaming and figuring out new avenues to greatness. However, they often lack the tools to develop those ideas into workable activities. Parents can improve the horizons for young people by making sure they have loads of experiences. Take them everywhere and let them experience life as you experience it. The cleaners, grocery stores, the auto mechanic's shop…are great places where kids can learn how to deal with others, how to see things from others' perspectives. It becomes a laboratory for learning from the most important person in their life—you.

Give your children varied materials to read. Whether it's comic books, graphic novels or maybe preteen magazines, reading any of those will improve their literacy. Remember, it really doesn't matter what they read as long as you read with them and help them understand the context and text of the writings. Make sure your kids have a lot of friends from different walks of life so they can learn how life works. You have to expose them to life. Parents want to keep their kids safe and secure, but they have to know how to relate to others and realize that the world is not a monolith. Life is diverse, real and alive and they have to learn to navigate it.

Parents must remember they have to give children the gift of confidence. And give them the freedom to make mistakes and fail within the confines of the family structure. Tell your children every day how precious they are and how special they are to you.

Let them know that often you must go it alone. When you have an idea that goes against the grain of conventional thought, you must be prepared to charge forward with nothing but your personal conviction and faith in your vision.

It's best if you have friends with you when you come up with a solution to a problem. That way, grief and glory can be shared. You must see what it is you want. It has to be crystal clear in your active and passive mind.

Chapter 2

*Doing the Rèsearch and
Narrowing the Focus*

In putting on a bake sale designed to repair the playground, I was taking on a task I had never done before. I had questions as to how I would start. Also, if I started the journey, would anyone take me seriously?

When searching for solutions to problems, one must use every resource possible to get information. The Internet is critical, but it is not the only source for information. Friends, adults, parents, and teachers have purviews that offer diverse views. That diversity is important in order to see all sides of an issue.

My parents told me to start by using the information and the common sense I already possessed. Words of wisdom I had received from teachers and friends were another starting point. Even the reports I had written in the third and fourth grades would come in handy. I guess this was proof that they were right. I remembered the strategy Ms. Causley taught me on how to get started doing research on topics new to us. So I got my note cards out and began to plot out the key words, likely articles, book titles and possible topics. Then I moved onto the trusty Safari, Google, Firefox, CHROME and other internet search engines, and let them do their job.

The first question I asked was "Has anyone else ever faced this problem and were they able to solve it?" We often think we are the only one who has ever had a problem. But more often than not, somewhere among the three billion people in the world, somebody has seen and solved the problem before.

After researching how to solve the problem, the second question is whether or not it can be solved with your skills and current resources. The third question is whether the solution is physically, conceptually and operationally possible—this is the "will" question. Do you and your team have the will, the energy and the desire to pull it off? If the answer to all three is yes, then the "do-ability" test has been answered in the affirmative.

Look closely at how others solved the problem. Examine the steps they took and ask whether you can replicate the steps. Can you do the same thing? While you may not be able to copy the steps, you may be able to gain a better understanding of the problem and possible solutions from their experience. Their strategy might be the right strategy and the tools utilized might be the right ones.

Ask the following questions:

1. If they did fix it, how did they do it and how long did it take?

2. What were the shortfalls?

3. What resources were necessary to get it done?

4. What were the lessons learned from the experience?

5. What resources did they have?

6. What were the pitfalls?

7. When they had failures, what did they do?

8. Once they completed their task, how did it work?

9. Take all this information and write on the wall— DON'T REINVENT THE WHEEL!

My father and I watched a movie entitled *The Patriot* (2000). In an early scene, the father tells his son when shooting at a target, "aim small, miss small." I have made my motto to focus on the target and if I miss the center of the target, at least try to come close to it.

Young people are often afraid of their ideas. They need much support to believe in themselves and their ability to figure things out. What they need most are the tools for doing so. Parents and teachers must give children the opportunity to fail and fail often without judgment. Let your children explore, think and figure things out on their own. Then guide them to perfection.

Then, when conducting do-ability testing on their ideas,

they have to be shown how to go to the edge of the cliff without falling off or jumping off when things don't go right.

It is important for young people to develop their analytical and problem solving skills in various settings. Adults can help them practice a broad range of analytical tasks having them put together puzzles, play group board games or complete computer gaming activities. However, it is important to encourage them to translate that newly developed skill set to real life situations.

Chapter 3

Plotting the Strategy and
Taking Bold Decisive Steps

W e are all afraid of failure; some of us are even afraid of success. But the only way to reach our goals in life is to take bold and decisive steps in the right direction. You can't be concerned with how things have always been done or using the tried and true methods. Sometimes you just have to create your own reality of what will be rather than what is or was. But you have to think it through before you begin this journey.

If you want to reach a goal, you have to plot a strategy that can be seen by others and is attainable. Remember, the strategy begins and ends with the goal. You start with visualizing what the completed task will look like. You examine the strengths and weaknesses of the strategy, paying close attention to where things might fall apart.

The strategy should be able to be reduced to a graphic—a picture or an organizational chart. All effective planning strategy works from the end to the beginning. When participants can see a chart or some kind of graphic that represents the path they are taking, they more clearly understand their roles. Doing it that way helps to develop a logic model and a sense of how the task should be done. When the graphic is not available, some groups lose sight of the goal as they go through the process. If that occurs and difficulty arises, they begin making it up as they go along.

Once you are clear on the possibility and the framework for accomplishing the tasks, take bold, decisive steps to accomplish it. Find the biggest obstacle and run to it in order to see exactly how immovable it is. You will often be surprised to find that the most difficult problems are smaller than you thought they were. In solving the large issues, the smaller ones become even smaller.

Another strategy is to bite off a little more than you can chew, and then ask others to help. There is an old Kentucky saying that says, "If you have a big problem, you have to get a lot of people around it." Using this big-problems-get-a-big-crowd philosophy provides a reason to get skilled members of the group to work with you to solve problems. This strategy allows you to take even bolder steps and more decisive actions that will lead to quick problem resolution. More importantly, it requires you to involve others in the process.

It's often good to create a flowchart of how you are going to go about achieving the end result. This helps you see the plan from start to completion of the project.

When working with young people, it is important to let them explore. They need to have a sense that you support their dreams and desires; they need to know that if they fail, it is all right and that you will be there to show them how to succeed.

I am not a believer that failure always leads to success. Sometimes failure leads to more failure. Kids need to be free to fail, but you can't help them practice failure. Help them develop the right habits that lead to success and then give them opportunities to practice success more often than failure. Teach them that lemonade was the objective of lemons—not the sour taste they leave when eaten in their natural state.

Chapter 4

Painting a Landscape
Tinged With Nirvana

What I hadn't counted on in the bake sale experience was my classmates not agreeing with me. I wondered how they could see something different that what I saw. We were all the same age; I assumed we all had the same experiences. But that was not true; it is never true. As a leader you have to understand that people bring a history of differing experiences. Those different experiences color how they see the world and how they go about solving problems.

Everyone is not the same and doesn't have the same sense of urgency about the same things, and everyone can't see the same vision. Where you see red, they see green; where you see up, they see down. Not only is this disconcerting for a leader, it is downright perplexing. Leaders need to realize that people won't always agree with you and at the end you won't always get what you want.

There is such a thing as leadership ego and it often clouds a leader's view of the world. Leaders sometimes assume that leadership knows best and should be agreed with at all costs. But unless it is a group of one, individuals in a group each have their way of seeing the world, shaped by the environment that shaped their experiences and their acquaintances. Leaders often feel that they can will others to see the same vision as they have or that the group can be forced to go along with what the leader says. The task of leadership is to paint a picture of what can be that merges the hopes and desires of the group. The final task is to let the group see themselves in the completed picture. This strategy illustrates and displays the vision, then encourages others to see themselves in the completed picture. So you have to paint a landscape that is familiar to them.

I had to establish a vision of what we all saw in a way they could imagine it. They had to feel comfort and familiarity in the picture that I was creating. Remember you must paint the picture but don't color in all the spaces. That's for them to do.

In developing this skill with children, it is important to build upon the things they know. Begin with their interests, and then broaden them, ever expanding on what excites them. Challenge them to take the lead in showing you the things they think are important and ask them for more information. Together, explore the unknown and let them lead the way.

Chapter 5

Getting the Others
to Line Up

When kindergarten children go on a walking field trip, the teacher takes out a knotted rope and asks each student to line up and take hold of a knot on the rope and proceed in single file. While on their trek, students may meander, turn around, joust with one another, but they never let go of the rope.

Why do they hang onto the rope? Is it because they have no concept of what a line is and must have a physical reminder? Or could it be that they want to make sure they are going where everybody else is going and where the leader is taking them? Perhaps they are obedient followers, willing to follow the lead of someone who seems to know where they are going.

Whatever the motivation, they usually arrive at the predetermined destination on time, intact, and together.

Some of them have traveled blindly and some of them have observed the path to the goal, but most importantly, they all arrived together. So ultimately the teacher's guide rope kept them moving in the same direction.

This knot-in-the-rope strategy is a great strategy when leaders attempt to get others to follow them into the unknown. The group sees the starting point and they see the goal; they know that the shortest distance between two points is a straight line. But they are unable to move in that straight line together without some of them veering off in another direction. So you have to create ropes, guideposts, and checkpoints to help the group see its way to the goal and assure them that they are moving in the same direction.

To provide the guidepost, leaders have to constantly give feedback to every individual because every person has his or her own ideas and thoughts on how something should be done. Also, leaders must positively assure the group of their progress toward the goal to help satisfy their fears. They need to know they are doing what is expected of them and they need to be celebrated when they are moving in the right direction. Praise them for keeping their hands glued to the rope and heading in the same direction toward the goal.

The caution here is to figure out how and when to tell them if they are moving in the wrong direction without impeding their desire to continue to move forward. This is a delicate process that demands coercive energy. It means you have to deflect their negative comments about you as the leader and accept some of the blame. You must allow them to save face and move beyond the immediate problem.

Every solution must be about the group; it is critical to establish positive groupthink about goal attainment.

Remember that in any group there will be naysayers, who believe the goal is unattainable; sightseers, who are oblivious to what is going on—they are just holding on to the rope and being led; and visitors from outer space, who are not even on the same page with the group. Remember, everybody is on the same goal trip—your job is to get him or her there.

When working with young people, you must continue to develop the sense of working in teams. Kids need to recognize that in every organization there are power struggles and there are times when people just don't get along. When this occurs, one has to work through it and persevere. Team sports, team games, group rewards and group punishment are a great way to establish the notion that one must always pay attention to everyone and their betterment.

Ultimately, young people must develop a sense of co-dependence for group success. They have to understand that just as the body has a number of parts that work together for a more unified and successful whole, so do groups as they work together to find success.

Chapter 6

*Working Through Doubt
and Never Being Afraid*

So the Good Book my parents read daily says, "Now faith is the substance of things hoped for, and the evidence of things not seen" (Hebrews 11:1 KJV). As I have worked with others, I have found that faith is the key. A leader must have faith in the abilities of individuals and see each of them as a partner working toward the goal. The leader must have faith in their talent, in their judgment, in their decision-making and in the group's commitment to reaching the goal. Remember, it is the evidence of things not seen that is the tough part.

Sometimes, in a group the doubt is palpable and it manifests itself with anger, whining, derisive behavior or individuals walking away. The goal of the leader is to have individuals keep the faith in themselves and each other while they are striving to reach the goal. This means you have to talk and talk and talk to them about the vision/goal and where they are in relationship to it. They have to have the sense that they are moving toward it at a meaningful pace.

Leaders have to realize that there is no success without working through the doubt and that doubt happens every day, even, to the leaders. So wake up each morning and ask what can go wrong, what has gone wrong, what might go wrong and what are the possible solutions. By thinking through those issues each day, you can develop strategies and possible solutions before the problems arise.

All of us have the demon of failure nipping at us; it is a remembrance of times past when everything went wrong or when everything fell apart. There are times when an individual questions his or her own abilities or the resolve of the group. The only way to exorcise those demons is to admit they exist and confidently strategize through them. Trust in your ability to see clearly through the fog of doubt. The goal that was in front of you a moment ago is still there, if you move forward.

Young people need to recognize there is more than one way to reach a goal. Most of them already know there is more than one way to do a math problem and there are different ways to tell a story. Young people should be given practice in developing alternatives to reaching their goal through board games such as Scrabble or other analysis and decision-making games.

Chapter 7

Working the Plan

You have to have a plan—a written plan that others can see, touch, and follow. The roughest part of any venture is following through. The plan must be a living plan; one that can change when circumstances call for changes in a process or changes in the goals. The circumstances are constantly changing and you must be ready for it. Everyone in the group must recognize the responsibility they have to review, reshape and approve the plan at every step along the way.

It may seem that in giving them that freedom, you have given them control of the organization. In reality, you are giving the group the responsibility to figure out the best way for them to be helpful and productive while achieving the goal. When the group is able to see the goal clearly and is reminded daily about their progress, they will work to find the best way to reach that goal—it will be in their self-interest.

Sometimes the best way to get people to follow the plan is to do as Dorothy did in the *Wizard of Oz* and just have them follow the yellow brick road. Most groups need a roadmap so they can chart their direction and mark their progress. The plan must have milestones and, upon reaching each milestone, the groups should review the progress and see if any adjustments to the plan are necessary.

My dad is always quoting a book called *Vertical Run*. There, the protagonist utters the watchwords "control the random element." This refers to an unspecified and unexpected occurrence that stands in the way of reaching the goal. Something always comes up; it is important to be on the lookout for it, when you see it, control it before it controls you.

Also, in all planning, leaders have to think about the carpenter's mantra to "measure twice, cut once." Meaning: Plan and then plan again to make sure everything has been taken care of to the best of the group's ability and then proceed.

Finally, leaders must execute, execute, execute. The difference between good leaders and great leaders often comes down to execution. No plan or strategy is worth anything if it is not executed. Leaders have to have a concrete plan, the resources necessary to execute the plan, the tools necessary for individuals to use, the budget to fund the activities and the energy to pull it off.

Young people are often so excited about what they are excited about that they forget there are steps to be followed before the goal can be reached. They live in a world of instant change, instant gratification, and multiple opportunities to change course. They haven't learned the word patience and have no idea what deferred gratification is all about. Adults have to give them multi-staged learning and gratification activities that show them how to accept small victories that lead to greater ones.

Chapter 8

Keeping Everyone Excited

If you don't have a cheerleader outfit, get one; because sometimes you have to cheer all by yourself. In the beginning of new adventures, everyone in the group seems to be excited; they rally around the idea of doing something that has never been done. They relish in the prospect of being in the vanguard of newness and seem to share in the excitement of the moment. But as time moves on and the euphoria wanes, both real and imaginary problems arise.

Sometimes, individuals external to the group raise questions. Their inquiries may cast doubt concerning the idea itself or the worthiness of the plan. At those times, the group wanders and also, may question the reason for coming together and whether or not the plan of action can be enacted. This doubt, brought on by others, often causes the group to become less enthused in their pursuit of the goal. This lethargy can be infectious, if not abated; it can be the starting point of a downward spiral of discontentment. This is when you break out the cheerleader outfit.

Also, each day there are new personal problems from home that affect members of the group and challenge the process. Sometimes sickness, sorrow and life get in the way and impact the work of the group. When this happens, there are often arguments; loud discussions occur that have nothing to do with what the group is trying to accomplish. Rather, they are just spillovers from life. Often at those moments nerves get frayed and the mood of the group takes a hit. Ultimately, things don't move along smoothly and nothing gets accomplished at the expected pace. Again, this is when you break out the cheerleader outfit.

As a leader, you have to stay in the moment. You have to make sure the obstacles you see in front of you that could impede your progress toward the goal are real and not just a mirage. Remember, all problems aren't of the same magnitude and are not of equal importance. Every problem does not have to be solved at the same time. You may be the only one who realizes that fact, so, it is important to tell the group often they there is nothing to fear.

Those around you need to be assured that the pathway is clear. They have to be empowered to maximize their energies toward solving the most pressing problems one at a time and then move on to the next problem. Discuss with them how often difficulties have arisen and they had achieved success in spite of them. If it is necessary to restructure the process or reorient the milestones, this is a good time to do it with each member involved in the discussion. No one likes to be in the dark alone, so, grab hands and walk them through this time together. Tell them, "The sun is always shining. It's just behind the clouds. Be positive, be nice and calm down." Members of the group need to know they are doing a good job; they need to be aware that they are getting closer to the goal.

Young people struggle with not getting what they want when they want to get it. Most of them have lived in a world of prepackaged food, on-demand entertainment and instant messaging. Taking their time to achieve a goal is not in their DNA and not an experience they have practiced. When things do not happen quickly, they get frustrated and act out. They get moody, throw tantrums and become dismissive of each other and adults. Remember they are young and don't have the experience to know how to handle is disappointment or defeat; giving up is often the only strategy many of them know.

Adults can help kids develop a capacity for patience and fortitude. As silly as it sounds, taking long walks and discussing what you see along the way gives young people an opportunity to slow their lives down and drink in the experience. Also, preparing dinner, step by step, rather than micro waving it allows young people to gain an appreciation of the process involved in reaching a goal. Find things that take time and take the time to do them, the rewards will be amazing and they will learn how to follow steps and the importance of doing so.

Often the best strategy for teaching patience and fortitude is to continually praise young people's progression as they move toward their goal. Everyone wants to know they are doing a good job and being productive. Most need an external compass to tell them when they are moving in the right direction. Often, even adults sometimes don't trust our own thoughts, young people are the same. So, praise them each step along the way as they pursue their goals. Put them on praise overload; soon they will believe you must be right. Remind them they are really good and all things are possible, if they keep working at it.

Chapter 9

Knowing When You Are Done

A friend of my parents once told them he had written fourteen books. None of them were on the bestseller list. He said some were better than others but none of them were earth shattering or changed the course of rivers—but they were all good enough. Good enough to be written, good enough to be read and good enough to be recognized by others as—good enough.

The goal is to have a plan, a strategy and a course of action that is good enough to reach the goal. Along the way, it is critical to know if you are moving in the right direction. Even when you don't want to know the truth, you have to have people around you who will tell you the truth about how things are going. You have to answer questions about whether the team is happy, whether there are enough resources, and whether you are moving down a path that will allow you to reach the goal in a timely manner, and whether you are correctly utilizing the plan you put into place.

Sometimes your gut tells you things are going badly, but the data might tell you something entirely different and vice versa. That means you have to review, assess and evaluate the process in order to clarify what is really happening. Often the passions of the moment have great influence over our emotions and can cause us to make decisions based on false assumptions.

But most importantly, you have to know when the task is done and when the goal has been reached. Most of us second-guess ourselves on every decision we make. We analyze everything and, given the time, we would readjust and reorganize ourselves into oblivion. The Reverend Martin Luther King Jr. called this the "paralysis of analysis."

It is good to review the plan, but it is also important to review the goals you have set. Everything changes, and sometimes circumstances, people and timing mandate augmentation of the goal. You might have to expand your thinking or pull back from what is really achievable with the resources or the time you have to accomplish the goal. Either way, it is important to recognize that the goal is sometimes a moving target.

When the bulls-eye of the goal is within sight, go at it with all your might. Make sure no teammate misses the sighting and celebrate its attainment together. As a leader, it is important for you to make sure that everyone knows they have reached the agreed-upon goal. There may be some who think that more should be done or that the group has gone too far. Nevertheless, celebrate the goodness of agreed-upon goal attainment.

In Chapters 3 and 4, I talked about focusing and working the plan. Imbedded in the plan should be measures or milestones that help you know if you are making the desired progress.

As you reach those milestones, mark them off together and move on to the next one. Remember, each task has to be completed first before moving on. When each milestone has been reached before moving on and the final task has been completed, you can feel confident that you are finished. Also, you can be assured, what you have accomplished is good enough.

Chapter 10

Requisites of Leadership

1. Have vision. The way to have vision is to read everything about everything (even when it is topics that only boys want to read about). You must broaden your outlook on life, people and everything. Talk to a lot of people and be interested in what they have to say, even when the topic is boring. Most of all, keep dreaming.

2. Trust yourself, but listen to the smart people around you. Self-doubt is a downer. Whenever it rears its ugly head, smash it down with a sledge hammer. Never doubt your resolve, never doubt your vision, and never doubt your ability to get things accomplished. Depend upon yourself for success. Depend upon others for help. There are smart people on your team; they know more than you do about something that is important to the process—listen to them. Remember, you can't delegate your dream to someone else.

3. Go with your gut; listen to your heart. Go with your passions. Do the things you care deeply about and have an interest in seeing through to the end. When developing strategies and selecting partners to help you use logic, at the end of the day, when decisions are difficult, trust your gut. Your past experiences, what you know, what you have been told and karma will lead you in the right direction when all else fails.

4. Hear dissenting voices around you. Dissenting voices are necessary because they allow you to see different perspectives. Listening to them helps to balance your perspective and guide your way. That doesn't mean you have to do what the dissenting voices say to do, but listen to them. There is logic, sound or not, in the position taken. But listen and use your logic and your gut to make a decision.

5. Include others and reframe your ideas to achieve consensus. Individuals need to hear their voices along the way. They need to know they are valued and are part of the solution. As a leader, always listen. While you are listening, reshape and reframe the ideas others have in a way that fits the strategies earlier developed. Discuss the ideas of group members and allow them to modify good ideas and adopt great ones. The goal is to keep moving along the straight line, or as straight a line as possible. Doing so leads to success and goal attainment.

Remember: While you may be a singular genius, there are other geniuses in the group. Gaining support from them allows the genius quotient to improve exponentially.

6. Trust people in your group, even when they don't trust themselves. Chain link fences are durable, expansive, flexible and strong. But they really are only as strong as the weakest link. The task in leadership is making sure that the weakest link is as strong as the strongest link.

All individuals in the group come with their own fears that cause them to doubt their abilities and question those of others. The flip side of the coin is they have enormous strengths and when one capitalizes on those, the strengths of the group clearly outweigh the weaknesses. Trust their strengths, and let them know you trust them. Put them in positions where success is possible and trust their ability to continue that success.

7. Learn to execute and don't cheat the process. You have to plan the work and work the plan. Always make a detailed plan and share that plan with everyone every day. Individuals' memories are not good as we think they are and they forget things over night. So early and often remind them where they are going, how they are going to get there, what the plan is, what their role is, what the role of others is and how they interconnect in order to reach the goal.

Also, don't cheat the process. In baseball there are four bases and even when you hit a home run you must touch all four. There is comfort in touching all the bases before reaching home plate; the ninety feet between each base provides for a growing sense of accomplishment as each one is touched. Don't cheat the player from experiencing the grandeur of those feelings as well as the lessons learned.

8. Don't let them see you sweat. Leadership is about leading. As my parents say, it is about getting people to do things they would not ordinarily do. They won't follow you if they see you sweat. While you may be lost in the fog, stay above the clouds and keep your eyes glued to the potential of reaching the goal. Know that your fears are real, your frustrations are sane, and the sense of doom is foreboding. Keep them to yourself.

9. Give everybody credit. Everyone in the group contributed something, even if it was just their presence. Sometimes it seems that because some have put in more time or were more energetic, they deserve more accolades. In reality, the wind beneath everyone's wings is everybody else. Good, bad or indifferent, members of the group have all pushed and pulled to success.

10. Know when good enough is good enough. Always know when good enough is good enough. There is always the temptation to think things through too much, to push toward idealized perfection. Always know when the goal has been reached. Constantly evaluate whether or not you have reached your goal; be aware where you are based on your goal and what is really necessary to be completed for success. They are not always the same.

Bonus: There is a more excellent way. It is important to know that the problem you worked so hard to solve will raise its ugly head again in life. As a leader, always think about how you might approach it differently when it does arise. Pay attention to group responses, review how they responded along the way and measure against your leadership effort. The next time this or similar problems arise, you will have a better response to it.

Finally, people create problems and people must solve them. No matter what the issue, people—not circumstances or technology—probably created the problem and people made the condition worse. People are the ones charged with finding a solution. The charge of leadership is to get people to work harmoniously. Then strike a chord of confidence leading them to success.

Tomorrow's Leaders

Tomorrow's leaders will be different from today's leaders. They will be more culturally sophisticated, ethnically diverse and globally oriented, with a view toward international peace and sustainability. They will be transformative in their vision and approach to facing the challenges of the twenty-first century. Already, they understand the need to create new paradigms for addressing many of the issues of conflict that grieve today's national and international communities.

How does one develop this kind of leadership talent among young people? By affording them the opportunity to grow academically in a challenging environment steeped with analytical and cultural expanding experiences; by challenging them with the great issues of the day; and giving them the chance to debate and bring solutions to domestic and international issues as they see them. Through these experiences that seek to harness the inherent leadership talents they already possess, they will broaden their perspectives, develop new skill-sets and improve their communication abilities.

About the Author

Taylor Wilson Thompson is a high school student in Chicago who has been passionate about encouraging young people to take on leadership roles in society. When she was ten years old, she received a leadership award at her school and attended the Junior National Leadership Conference in Washington D.C. Those experiences kindled her enthusiasm about being a young leader and she was determined to inspire others her age. She created the Taylor Wilson Thompson Family Fund (twtff.org) as a way to encourage leadership development at the middle and high school grade levels. She has partnered with numerous schools across the country to develop models for leadership development. An avid reader and writer, she has written this book as a means to add greater voice to her mission.

www.ingramcontent.com/pod-product-compliance
Lightning Source LLC
Chambersburg PA
CBHW071642050426
42443CB00026B/870